Pearls of Hope
with
Stress Solutions for the Soul

A 31Day Guide on Tools for Life

Edie Hand
And
Lauren E. Miller

Please Note: On many of the pages we have
included areas for you to share your feelings,
and to make notes about portions of the book
you want to remember.   Feel free to
personalize this book in those areas to
highlight passages that have special meanings
for you.

Lauren and Edie

Copies of this book can be purchased
at any of these websites

Amazon.com

LaurenEMiller.com

EdieHand.com

ISBN-13: 978-8-218-63154-3

I dedicate this book to my son, Linc Hand, my God son Jonathan Flowers, my chosen family, and to all my friends who have helped me dance through the storms.

To my biggest encourager, Colleen Ruszkowski , a true earthly sister that brings much joy to my seasoned life.

Grateful to God and his amazing Grace.
Edie

I dedicate this book to my parents, John and Kay Miller, thank you for teaching me how to seek the blue sky beyond the clouds.

I love you,
Lauren

Welcome to Pearls of Hope, Stress Solutions for the Soul; A 31Day Guide to a Fuller Life

Edie Hand, international author, television personality, radio host, and founder of The Edie Hand Foundation has teamed up with Lauren E Miller, founder of Stress Solutions University.com to share with readers these short meditations and reflections to help you remember what your soul already knows.

You are beautiful and wonderfully created in the image of God; you are safe and capable of handling any situation that unfolds before you.

We hope the following phrases, prayers and insights expand your ability to remember your God given natural state of being: a joy-filled, peaceful, loving, creative and solution based spiritual being having an earthly experience.

If you have ever given worry, doubt and fear more authority in your life than God then this book will build your spiritual skills to help you access and apply your greatest source for personal excellence in life which is your relationship with your Creator.

Day 1: The Disease to Please

What if you could go through your day without the fragmentation of thinking "what will people think?" Are you caught up in the disease to please?

Tomorrow morning before you step into your day take a few moments to seek clarity before God around the purpose for which your heart beats for that day of life you have been gifted with. Ask yourself: "Why am I doing what I do?"

Once three specific insights around that question emerge, align yourself with what you value most and stay focused.

Rising and falling emotionally is the result of your concern around what others will think.

Two revealing questions to explore:

How much of what you do in your day is because of who you are before God?

How much of what you do in your day is to be seen, acknowledged and recognized by those around you?

You may say some days, "well, I don't know what I feel called to do." When this is the case remember that one of your consistent callings, as a human being is to grow in the ways of love and kindness

1

each day. That is deathbed wisdom. Enjoy the process of growth!

Dear God,
Have your way with me today in spite of myself because I know your way results in a peace that passes all human understanding. Fill me with a desire to please only you so that my purpose gains clarity, more today than yesterday.

Pearl of Hope:

Changing how we feel is more difficult than changing how we think or how we behave.
If change is all there is, choice is all we have.

That is the way we see it.

Day 2: Ignore the Voices of Doubt

"For I know the plans I have for you, declares the Lord. Plans to prosper you and not to harm you, plans to give you hope and a future."
Jeremiah 29:11

Gripping onto the wheel of life? Consider releasing your grip this week and ignore the voices that evoke fear, doubt & worry: "While Jesus was still speaking, some men came from the house of Jarius the synagogue ruler. 'Your daughter is dead,' they said. 'Why bother the teacher any more?' IGNORING what they said, Jesus told the synagogue ruler, 'Don't be afraid; JUST BELIEVE" Mark 5:35-36

Dear God,

Fill me up with a courageous faith that chooses to believe against all odds. I too want to be able to ignore the voices of doubt and give belief permission to have its way in my thought life. As I lean my entire personality into your definitive purpose for my life I trust that my way will be filled with love and confidence.

Pearl of Hope:

No matter what the season never stop dreaming. Give your God inspired passion, perseverance and positive projection permission to guide your ride.

That is the way we see it.

Day 3: Flexibility = Strength

Did you know when trees are buffered by the wind they crack and sap fills in the gaps making it more flexible when hit by the next gust of wind. God speaks through nature...I literally just climbed a pine tree and witnessed this simple truth first hand. As you move through the gusty winds in life remember you will be left with the ability to endure. Everything is sent to make you fearless don't shrink back from the opportunity to remember your God given strength to overcome!

Dear God,

I pray for the ability to remain flexible and unattached to the work of my hands. I know the more attached I am to the outcomes in life the less flexible I become. I want to be able to move quickly in life to where ever the Holy Spirit sends me. Grant me the grace of release and flexible responses to everything that will unfold today.

Pearl of Hope:

One of my mugs has this printed on the side: Don't Quit

When things go wrong, as they sometimes do, remember that failure is simply a label we place on undesirable outcomes. When the road you are trudging seems all uphill, when the funds are low and debts are high, and you want to smile but you have to sigh. When care is pressing you down a bit, rest if you want...but don't you quit.

Life is strange with its twists and turns, as every one of us sometimes learns, don't give up though the pace seems slow, you might succeed with another blow, success is failure turned inside out.

As Vince Lombardi said: "Winners never quit and quitters never win."

That is the way we see it.

Day 4: What Has Mastered You?

2 Peter 2:9 "A man is enslaved by whatever has mastered him."

This is a very intriguing verse in that it invites you to consider those things in life that you have farmed out your sense of identity to. For example, greed (a selfish and excessive desire for more of something) has many faces: money, affection, attention, status, recognition, respect, knowledge, popularity, control. What is your muse? What enslaves you in life? Perhaps you simply notice a downcast feeling when you do not get a desired outcome. View this feeling as an invitation to explore releasing your need for a specific situation in order to know you have already 'made it' or to give yourself the gift of love and acceptance no matter what happens around you. This is worth a moment of your attention. For it is in the light of revelation that you resurrect your ability to release that which has gained an unhealthy grip on you in life.

The cool thing is, you are the one who farmed out your identity to that which has enslaved you, which means you are fully equipped to take back your power. Surrender all to God and peace will return, along with your ability to step into your fullest God given potential to create and inspire, without the heavy shadows of distraction like greed and envy.

Dear God,

I desire to be mastered only by you for you fashioned me after your own heart so my greatest joy and peace rests only in and through you. As Mother Teresa used the example of a fish in water, no matter what space I move in today, you surround me.

Pearl of Hope:

Let us strip off every weight that slows us down. As you let go of the non-essentials in life, you create more room for the essential, those things you value most and that are aligned with your highest good and the good of all concerned. Lighten your load by spring cleaning items in your life that do not align with what you value most...including a negative thought life.

That is the way we see it.

Day 5: I Am

When Moses asked God, "Who Should I say sent me?" God replied,

"I Am". 'I Am' is a declaration of identity. God is the great I Am omnipresent creator of life. YOU are created in his image and have the same ability to create your reality through your thoughts which create your words which create your perceived reality. Stay awake at the gate of your thoughts.

Be very careful of your choice of words after 'I Am' or 'My' statements. What ever you choose to put after those statements becomes linked to your sense of identity.

Instead of:

I Am sick

I Am exhausted

I Am overwhelmed

My tremor

My illness

My pain

My lonliness

My negative thoughts

Try speaking these:

I Am a child of God, ALL things are possible for me

I Am healthy

I Am energized

I Am capable of coming up with creative solutions

I Am strong

I Am joyful

I Am loving

I Am grateful

My ability to succeed

My ability to heal

My ability to create positive, healthy relationships

My ability to focus on what is working out for me

Stay AWAKE at the GATE of your thoughts knowing they form your spoken words. Your body follows the commands you speak which create your perspectives on life which become your reality.

Dear God,

I give you permission to stand watch at the gate of my thoughts. Should any negative, self-defeating or judgmental thought slither out of my mind's gate slay it quickly.

Pearl of Hope:

We should remember to always respond to situations instead of reacting to them. Take the high road.

That is the way we see it.

11

Day 6: What Seed are You?

In Matthew 13:18-23 Jesus says:

"Listen then to what the parable of the sower means: When anyone hears the message about the kingdom and does not understand it, the evil one comes and snatches away what was sown in their heart. This is the seed sown along the path. The seed falling on rocky ground refers to someone who hears the word and at once receives it with joy. But since they have no root, they last only a short time. When trouble or persecution comes because of the word, they quickly fall away. The seed falling among the thorns refers to someone who hears the word, but the worries of this life and the deceitfulness of wealth choke the word, making it unfruitful. But the seed falling on good soil refers to someone who hears the word and understands it. This is the one who produces a crop, yielding a hundred, sixty or thirty times what was sown."

Pulling from Jesus parable of the sower, be aware of these 3 things: worldly anxiety, the lure of riches and the cravings for things. They choke out your awareness of your God given mission on earth (to grow in the ways of love and use the gifts you have been blessed with for a greater good). For from these flow jealousy, comparison, envy and selfish ambition which block your ability to access your fullest God given potential & life experience to create to inspire.

Dear God,

Increase my discomfort when I am caught up in worldly anxiety, riches and cravings. Replace my unsatisfied state with the awareness that only you can satisfy my deepest longings. Protect me from the habit of following the shiny objects in life that distract me from what is truly essential for interior joy and peace.

Pearl of Hope:

Stress is simply the power you give to outside circumstance to define your worth, value and what you believe you are capable of handling successfully.

That is the way we see it.

Day 7: Bloom Where You are Planted

"Therefore we do not lose heart. Though outwardly we are wasting away, yet inwardly we are being renewed day by day. For our light and momentary troubles are achieving for us an eternal glory that far outweighs them all. So we fix our eyes not on what is seen, but on what is unseen. For what is seen is temporary, but what is unseen is ETERNAL."
2 Corinthians 4:16-18

Take it from the bulb in the dark throughout the winter months. If it ever forgot its natural state of being, to bloom in this world, it would have ceased to emerge out of the darkness into the light.

There are no challenges in life only situations that invite us to remember our God given ability to come up with creative solutions...and move mountains.

Dear God,

Help me to embrace the challenges in life with eager expectation that I will gain a necessary character trait that I will need in order to handle the expansion you are guiding me into in life. May I bloom with love, gratitude and kindness no matter where you plant me today.

Pearl of Hope:

Steps to Shift Your Perspective in a Positive Direction:

1. *Trust that God is for you and is working on your behalf for a greater good: Be Unattached*
2. *Focus on what is working out for you versus what is not: Be Grateful*
3. *Implement Self-care systems that support your health and wellness*

That is the way we see it.

Day 8: Conditional Kindness

"Be kind to each other, tenderhearted, forgiving one another, just as God through Christ has forgiven you." Ephesians 4:32

Is Your Kindness Conditional?

It's easy to be kind when others are kind to you. Authentic godly character appears when a kind response is given in the face of a bitter remark. I practiced a kind response recently in spite of the raging ego within who almost got its way with my choice of words & intonation. I stand in awe at how the smallest flicker of kindness can dispel the dark shadows of bitterness. When priorities are clear decisions are easy...God first, people then tasks. When I forget what I value most in a moment of unbridled ambition, anxiety has its way in my body. Choose your responses wisely even if you have to act your way into feeling. Random acts of kindness lower the stress hormone and boost serotonin levels.
Be what you want to experience in life.

Dear God,

It's easy to be loving and kind to those who are loving and kind to me. I want the kind of love and ability to be kind that remains in tact no matter what threatening situation I find myself facing today. Help me to love for the sake of love along with confidence that love evokes more love and kindness evokes more kindness in this world. I want to be kind and loving because of who I am in you not because people are loving and kind to me.

Pearl of Hope:

Random acts of kindness are to service others without expecting anything in return.

That is the way we see it.

Day 9: Do You Believe?

In Mark chapter 9 Jesus encounters a man whose son is possessed. Basically this man asked Jesus, *"If you can do anything help us"* to which Jesus replied in Mark 9:23: *"If you can? EVERYTHING IS POSSIBLE for him who believes."* Do you believe in your capabilities? This is an essential ingredient for your creativity to be birthed into this world. Be congruent with your values and beliefs: Why are you doing what you are doing in this world?

If you align yourself with what you value most then your life will unfold with ease and grace. Stop looking for that which you can only find within. Live from the inside out today. God believes you can...do you?

Dear God,

Too often I grovel at the foot of the cross pleading for my request to be heard and crying out, "If you can do anything, help me." I often feel a heavenly push back at this approach because it is void of remembrance that whatever you call me to in this life you promise to give me the resources to do it successfully. Never once through my dark night of the soul experiences have you left me empty handed. Help me this day to remember the simple truth that all things are possible for those who believe. I believe Lord; help my unbelief.

Pearl of Hope:

Every great achievement was once impossible. Faith is like steel used to reinforce and strengthen concrete. Steel provides a strong foundation on which to build a desired structure. Faith provides a stable foundation on which to build a desired life structure along with living systems that support inner joy and peace. These all create an interior world that honors the person you desire to be. When you walk day by day in faith, it expands into more faith and life unfolds with ease and grace. Think about this, no matter what situation you find yourself in. If you truly believe in your heart of hearts that God has your best interest in mind for your ultimate good and the good of all concerned then fear, doubt, and worry are eliminated from your mental radar.

That is the way we see it.

Day 10: The Flow of Definitive Purpose

"Praise the Lord, O my Soul; all my inmost being praise his holy name...who redeems your life from the pit & crowns you with Love & Compassion." Psalm 102:1,4

" If I have the gift of prophesy, and know all mysteries and all knowledge; and if I have all faith, so as to remove mountains, but have not love, I am nothing." 1 Corinthians 13:2

Again I am reminded this morning of how essential the choice for love & compassion is when it comes to the experience of purpose. No matter what you think, create, say or pursue in this world if it is void of love & compassion as the essential fuels behind it all...it will come to nothing at the sunset of this life.

Are your thoughts, words and actions aligned with what you value most in this life? Are not the moments that linger in your past accessible to your conscious memory because you either have or have not experienced love & compassion?

Be that which you desire to experience around you today: If it's motivation, be a motivator. If it's positivity, then be positive in word, intonation, thought & deed. If it's compassion and forgiveness, then be compassionate and forgive along with avoiding slander. If it's the experience of open doors, then open doors for those around you. If it's love, then infuse love into your thoughts, words & deeds. Love & Compassion are woven into your God given natural state of being. A sense of purpose emerges within when you pursue and live out these attributes in your daily life.

Dear God,

Help me to live in love and for love so that my words, thoughts and actions flow with compassion and light up the work you call me to do today.

Pearl of Hope:

Teach me to act firmly and wisely, without embittering and embarrassing others. I want to love and serve first and then lead.

That is the way we see it.

Day 11: Forget the Past Make Room for the Now

"Forget the former things; do not dwell on the past. See, I am doing a new thing! Now it springs up; do you not perceive it? I am making a way in the desert and streams in the wasteland." Isaiah 43:18-19

Let go of your grip on your past desert and wasteland so that your hands and heart will be open to receive the refreshment that comes with the choice to begin again with God, celebrating the uniqueness of God's creative, loving Spirit which is your natural state of being.

Shake the desert and wasteland off, look up to the right (access the creative part of the brain) and ask for what you want and align it with what God delights in: love; joy; peace; patience; kindness; goodness; gentleness and self-control Stop lingering in needing to know why things happened as they did, be here now and open your heart up to the joy in the present moment. God said, I Am, not I was or I will be. Your greatest sense of being comes when you remove the distraction of past and future.

What do You value most in this life? Clarity of focus leads to accuracy of response. When you spend time thinking about, spending time with and pursuing what you value most you will experience more of it in your life. Whatever you choose to do in this world give it 100% of your effort, even if you find yourself in a place of transition. When you put forth 100% towards that which you happen to be doing NOW you can't help but swing open the doors to opportunity and possibilities.

Dear God,

I pray for the grace to be here now all day long. When I begin to drift into my past or run ahead to my imaginary future I give you permission to override the antics of my mind and bring me back to you in the moment that unfolds before me. Creativity and inspiration are uploaded in the NOW because that's where you dwell Lord...I want to stay in that space all day long.

Pearl of Hope:

Give God permission to help you forget the past and surrender the future. Embody and express God's divine love here and now in your thoughts, word and actions. With Gratitude, open your heart to learning and growing in the here and now. Seek to love and understand more than your desire to be loved and understood. Peace is your natural state of being when truth and presence prevail.

That is the way we see it.

Day 12: A Jesus Attitude

My prayer today is based off a scripture I read earlier this week that caught my attention, I believe that what God calls me to is possible now: "Your attitude should be the same as that of Jesus Christ " Phil 2:5

"God, I want the very mind of Christ as I go through another gift of life today. May I see, as he did, *You* in every face I encounter. Give me Jesus thoughts that were not imprisoned by the yoke of slavery to unbridled ambition for status or the unquenchable desire for approval. I want to choose love & compassion as Jesus did, over fear & judgment.

I want to think and respond as Jesus did: to love for the sake of love alone, untainted by hidden agendas or crevices of lack & scarcity. Break my heart over the things that broke yours as you walked the earth. I want to seek to understand over being understood, free from attachment to certain responses. Jesus existed above compliments & complaints, grounded in the purpose for which his heart beat: to be a missionary of love no matter what...I want that same energy and focus today. To be able to respond to criticism with even more love to make up for the lack of it in those moments. I believe this is my natural state of being so as you answer this prayer of mine my joy will be complete & my peace will be profound."

Pearl of Hope:

The key is to take one day at a time. Keep your prisoners of hopes near your mind and heart. God will give you restoration in due season.

That is the way we see it...

Day 13: Growth in the Midst of Condemnation

"This then is how we know that we belong to the truth, and how we set our hearts at rest in his presence whenever our hearts condemn us. For God is greater than our hearts, and he knows everything." 1 John 3:19-20

To condemn is to express a strong disapproval or indication that something is bad or wrong. When your heart condemns you, rejoice, it is a clear indication that you are spiritually discerning, awake enough within to recognize truth from falsehood. Awake enough within to identify actions that perhaps are tainted by ulterior motives fueled by selfish ambitions and vain conceits. It is in moments like this that you are invited to choose God above all distractions thereby returning to the fellowship that leads to profound wisdom and peace: your soul's connection to God.

Dear God,

Thank you for instilling within me the ability to discern what is good for me, and what is not. Increase my ability to recognize truth from falsehood; good from evil that I may gain ground today in a direction that moves me closer to you and the plans you have for me.

Pearl of Hope:

Today is about the White Pearl of second chances. At any time, you can release hurt or disappointment from your past whether it be self induced or the result of another person acting out their pain, you open yourself up to the experience of Psalm 51:10: "Create in me a pure heart, O God, and renew a steadfast spirit within me." Although you cannot change what happened yesterday, you can create a new spirit to begin a new day. Be ready to forgive and ask forgiveness, ready to release what was or what could have been and accept what is. Grace drops in now, not in the past or in the future. No matter your season in time, be willing to practice the art of letting go and giving yourself another chance to receive and begin again.

That is the way we see it.

Day 14: You're Not in This Alone

As the French Mystic Chardin said: you are first and foremost a spiritual being, having a physical experience.

"Not by might, not by power, but by my Spirit says the Lord." Zec 4:6

"Are you so foolish? After beginning with the Spirit, are you now trying to attain your goal by human effort?" Galatians 3:3

Trying to do things through your own efforts leads to mental and physical fatigue. Did you forget that God is with you?

Expand your awareness of the One who is Omnipresent, working through you to accomplish all things good, true and beautiful in this world.

Dear God,

Thank you that you promise to never leave me nor forsake me. I am grateful that I am never alone on this sometimes-challenging journey of life. Restore my ability to see and feel you walking closely by my side today. Help me to recognize the many different ways you will come to me today. I give my spirit permission to guide my flesh into all things today so that my strength will be expansive and my focus will be clear. May all that I do and say reflect my connection to you. Bless the work of my hands and heart and move the hearts of those who are meant to be moved to clear the path for me to go where you call me to go.

Pearl of Hope:

Clarity of focus leads to accuracy of response.

That is the way we see it.

Day 15: God is for You

"What, then, shall we say in response to this? If God is for us, who can be against us?" Romans 8:31

"Draw near to God and He will Draw near to You." James 4:8

Wake up and release your compulsion to watch others & draw conclusions about your current status (comparisons).

Authentic transformation that results in peace that passes all human understanding comes in Your Choice to become aware of God within you. As you wake up your awareness to your own thoughts, actions, motives & longings, you are in a position to direct them all back to God...who Will transform them back to your God given natural state of being: loving, peaceful, kind-hearted, creative & grateful.

Here in lies the true freedom you seek that has become disguised in your frantic pursuit of something that exists outside of you: status & the opinions of other people.

Dear God,

More of you today, less of me. May there be less lag time today than yesterday in my ability to hear and respond to the voice behind me saying, "This is the way, walk in it."

Pearl of Hope:

Action is often associated with hope and the decision for action can be hope generating itself. Feeling stuck? Take 1 positive action forward toward your desired goal. Say: God is with me and I am moving closer to a creative solution. The world is full of creative solutions; it is simply our perceptions that block our ability to tune into all of the options.

That is the way we see it.

Day 16: What Do You Value Most?

"The Lord our God, the Lord is one. Love the Lord your God with all your heart and with all your soul and with all your strength. These commandments that I give you today are to be upon your hearts. Impress them on your children. Talk about them when you sit at home and when your walk along with road, when you lie down and when you get up." Deuteronomy 6:4-7

Take a few moments to make a list of 5 things you value most in this life. Post this list in a place that you will frequently see throughout your day. As you reflect on this list ask yourself this question: Are my thoughts, words and actions in alignment with what I value most today?

I value people above things. When my actions are not aligned with this value then it is an opportunity for me to begin again. I also Highly Value my relationship with God. As I am gifted with each new day of life I will say, "God first, all things beautiful, good, right and true flow from this relationship in my life." Daily distractions lose their grip on you in life when you declare your commitment to honor what you value most. Having a definitive purpose leads to clarity of focus, inner peace and profound joy.

Remember, whatever you choose to focus on GROWS BIGGER.

Dear God,

Grant me the grace to tune into what I value most in the midst of my daily tasks. Move me to linger in those moments that add value to what is truly important in your eyes as I move forward today. Catch my attention in the midst of the mundane and lift my heart to heavenly contemplations.

Pearl of Hope:

Today, increase your capacity to receive. Be a mentor! You will reap what you sow.

That is the way we see it

Day 17: With God You Lack Nothing

"Those who have God, find they lack nothing. God alone suffices." St. Teresa of Avila

Watch out for EGO (Edging God Out) flare-ups. They kick in whenever you feel threatened by someone or something outside of you. They show up in the emotions of jealousy, anger, comparisons and self-doubt. Give God permission to have His way with you in spite of these flare ups as He reminds you of your unique value and purpose in this world, which includes the inner knowing that you are safe and lack nothing when you remain awake and aware of your connection to God. Release the shame that often emerges as you reflect on the moments you slip from your God given character into the baser emotions that flow from feelings of inadequacy. The fact that you are even aware and uncomfortable with the EGO flare ups is a clear indication of your spiritual acuity.

Today rather than edging God out look for ways to edge God in.

"Dear God, I give you permission to hold me close to your heart today. May I have one attachment: my heart to your heart, my thoughts to yours so that I grow in my abilities to act in accordance with your will which always shows up in love, kindness & confidence."

Pearl of Hope:

Create in me a pure heart and renew a steadfast spirit within me.
 Psalm 51:10

That is the way we see it.

Day 18: Irritation

"A soft answer turns away wrath, but a harsh word stirs up anger." Proverbs 15:1

Irritation in this life will often flow from your need to be right, seen, acknowledged, recognized, respected and responded to in a specific way . . . can you imagine giving these antics up and knowing you have already made it in this life?

God delights in you, no need for outside reinforcements. I would imagine we would have a lot of mind space freed up to create more love and beauty in this world . . . is not that the purpose for which we are graced with another heart beat?

Dear God,

When my heart is fixed on completing my "to-do" list I will too often over look precious opportunities to speak kindly and encourage those people you put in my path. The world screams and you whisper. Give me ears to tune into what you have to say. Reveal to me where you would have me go, what you would have me do in this gift of life you have blessed me with today. Recalibrate my focus so that what I do is void of selfish ambition and vein conceits fueled by the drug of approval. Help me to put people above things and to remember that I have already made it in your eyes.

Pearl of Hope:

Let us hold fast the confession of our hope without wavering. Be compassionate to your fellow mankind.

That is the way I see it

Day 19: Enthusiasm

"Remain in me, and I will remain in you. No branch can bear fruit by itself; Neither can you bear fruit unless you remain in me...I have told you this so that my joy may be IN you and YOUR joy may be COMPLETE." John 15:4,11

Enthusiasm is derived from the roots "en" and "theos" it means in (within) God, inspired by God and it's contagious.

In NLP they refer to a technique called eliciting states of behavior. Your choice of emotional expression each day will trigger
a similar response in those around you.

Dear God, you have created me with a heart that is full of passion and creativity. Thank you for the grace to bring this natural state of being to the front lines of my interactions today. It is my intention to live a life filled with YOU, with enthusiasm having full confidence that my choice to do so will push out apathetic responses and UnCork joy, laughter and abundant love...true wealth on this journey of life.

Pearl of Hope:

Studies continue to reveal that a positive attitude in life results in an increased life span, improved quality of life and many other health benefits.

That is the way we see it.

Day 20: Do What You Do Because of Who You Are

"How many are your works, O Lord. In wisdom you made them all; the earth is full of your creatures. There is the sea, vast & spacious, teeming with creatures beyond number-living things both large & small" Psalm 104:24-25

We think that if what we create is not seen acknowledged and recognized it has no value...not true. Consider the seas & the expansive reefs that have yet to be explored yet the character of God is revealed throughout the splendor of colors, textures & shapes even though no eye has beheld its glory.

It is because of God's nature that creation reveals such expansive beauty...And for no other reason.

How much of what you do is void of who you are because of your desire to be seen, acknowledged and recognized? Return to infusing all that you do with the Magnificent person you are and comparisons, jealousies & anxious desires will fall to the way side.

God did not say after creating the expansive, captivating beauty in creation, "This will be all worth it if someone sees it, acknowledges it and responds favorably to it." No, God created the expansive beauty and wonderment found throughout all of nature because of the very nature of who He Is...May it be the same for you...

As you create what you create without the need for applause, because that IS YOUR God given natural state of being, your creations will LIGHT UP THE WORLD.

Dear God,

Help me to do what I do and forget about it so that I have more mind space to tune into the next thing you have prepared for me to create.

Pearl of Hope:

When you do what you do because of who you are then all that you do will authentically light up the world around you without restriction.

That is the way we see it.

Day 21: The Drug of Approval

"Am I now trying to win the approval of men, or of God? Or am I trying to please men." Gal. 1:10

Step out of the drug of approval today: your need for recognition from others to know that what you do has value. God delights in you. Don't expect anything today except to be loved and cherished by God.

Dear God,

Thank you that I have the ability to remember that I am not what I do or what I have achieved. Who I am is a constant reality and flows from my identity in you, therefore, UNLESS I CHOOSE to farm out my sense of self worth and value to people, circumstances or situations, I will be free from the roller coaster that exists in the drug of approval.

If I do what I do to be seen by others then the drug of approval dilutes what I do and my authenticity is compromised. I choose this week to do what I do because of who I am, not because of how I want to be perceived.

Pearl of Hope:

When you know you are doing what you are born to do each day is filled with rainbows of hope.

That is the way we see it.

Day 22: Status & the Opinions of Other People

"Teacher, we know that you are a truthful man and that you are not concerned with anyone's opinion. You do not regard a person's status but teach the way of God in accordance with the truth." Mark 12:14

Jesus was never concerned about status or the opinions of other people, are you? These two pursuits too often rob us of inner peace and definitive purpose.

Dear God,

Thank you that my greatest source and fuel for happiness in this life occurs behind closed doors, when no one is watching...the prayers, dances, songs and free expressions of who I am before you alone.

I am willing to consider the freedom that Jesus Christ of Nazareth had when he walked the earth. Known as the Prince of Peace, he was not concerned about status or the opinions of other people.

This week I will explore letting go of my need to be seen, acknowledged and recognized in order to feel successful, loved and enough.

Fill me with an expansive Spirit of joy and laughter so that a levity around all things begins to emerge in all that I do and say.

I am grateful for another day to practice letting go of the non-essentials and nurture what I value most in this life.

Have your way with me in spite of myself...your way has never left me empty handed in this life.

Pearl of Hope:

Feel safe, connected and successful in and with God. Step out of a neediness for status and recognition.

That is the way we see it.

Day 23: Pride & Jealousy

"Love is patient, love is kind, it does not envy, it does not boast, it is not proud." 1 Corinthians 13:4

Jealousy flows out of pride. Pride occurs when you feel that you deserve to be respected by others. Pride fuels the feeling that you are more important than other people. Expectations on how you feel people should show up for you and frustration when they don't meet your expectations often leads to negative emotional outbursts. Because the nature of pride is to exalt itself above others it often gives birth to jealousy when encountering people it perceives to be more successful than itself. It is a dangerous reptile that wreaks havoc in our relationships and must be quickly replaced with love and humility so as to maintain healthy rapport with God and other people.

Dear God,

Thank you that I am not alone on this journey. Give me eyes to see, ears to hear and a heart to respond to the call for connection for a greater good in this world.

Remove from my mental radar all distractions of comparisons that breed pride or jealousy. Teach me to number my days aright that I may gain a heart full of wisdom and spend my moments creating what is good, right, beautiful and praise worthy...along with aligning what I do with who I am in You.

When people encounter me may they walk away ignited with You.

I am grateful that I woke up this morning and for another day to grow in the way of love, kindness and confidence.

Pearl of Hope:

True inner peace flows through the archway of humility, love and confidence. If God is for you, who or what can be against you. Remember, stress is simply the power you give to an outside circumstance to define what you believe you are capable of handling successfully. Take it back today.

That is the way we see it.

Day 24: Let Go and Let God

"Draw near to God and He will draw near to you."
James 4:8

Spiritual Practice: On a piece of paper write down those things in your life you are gripping ahold of and have yet to surrender to God...you know you have surrendered a situation to God when you no longer experience the sting of anxiety around it...FLIP the paper over and write, "I surrender all of this to You God" and then shred the paper.

When you experience an emotional anxiety flare up moment around that which you surrendered simply tap on your thymus located two inches down below the U-shaped dip in your neck and say: "No...delete...I choose God over this doubt, worry or fear."

Dear God,

I believe that you invite me each day into the experience of surrender, love and confidence with the gift of each new dawn.

I must admit, I can often feel interior seething along with protest when my soul calls me back to that place of letting go of my need to control, own, and possess.

A part of me says, "I need to grip onto this in order to get what I want in order to feel safe, successful or valued" in spite of the internal resistance on my part I give you permission today to have your way with me in spite of myself...because...

I have learned on this journey that I am never left empty handed when I make the choice to release my grip on life.

This choice to surrender all to You opens me up to receive more love and confidence as your divine gnosis seeps into my conscious awareness reminding me that you DO have plans to prosper and not harm me, to give me a hope and a future...along with the truth that your greatest gift to me is not that you prevent trials and hardships but you have the ability to bring about a GREATER GOOD than had the trial or hardship never occurred.

As you know so well, I have witnessed the above truth again and again and again...first hand, eye to eye, face to face.

Pearl of Hope:

Rather than ask, "why me?" Ask, "why not me?" and increase your confidence in the One who calls you into life. Trust that the necessary resources are available to you for solution based thinking as you learn and grow in earth school.

That is the way we see it.

Day 25: Anxiety & Fear

"Do not be anxious about ANYTHING, but in every situation, by prayer and petition, with thanksgiving, present your requests to God."
Philippians:4:6

"Take courage it is I, don't be afraid." John 6:20

Fear is simply a label we place on a situation we do not feel capable of handling.
Fear fuels anxiety in our life as we give more authority to our perceived threatening situation than we do to God. Consider that everything is sent to make YOU fearless in life. Shrinking back robs you of the chance to experience growth, understanding and love.

Don't voluntarily or deliberately worry. Stress is simply the power you give to outside circumstance to define your worth, value and capability. Jump in and adjust your perspective as soon as you become aware of it. Look your worry straight in the face and say:

"I see you for what you are a diluted perspective void of the remembrance that God is with me and ALL things are possible for me, ALL is well with my soul. I am capable of coming up with creative solutions in every situation, I simply forget that I am. Today, in this moment, I CHOOSE to remember and listen to the whisper of God verses the screams of the world reminding me that I TOO, like Peter,

can walk on top of water as long as I keep my eyes off of worry, doubt and fear."

Dear God,

Help me to give more authority to you over my fears, doubts and worries. I want to be able to hear your voice in the midst of my storm: "fear not, it is I." I willing to remember that with every challenge in life, you come too.

Pearl of Hope:

Steps to the Gift of Worry Free Living:

1. *Realize worry is counter-productive.*
2. *Accept what you lack control over: The Serenity Prayer: Dear God, give me the courage to change the things I can accept the things I can not change and the wisdom to know the difference.*
3. *Commit to positive change in thinking and actions.*
4. *Look for the good in each moment.*
5. *Always seek the opportunity for learning and growth: What is my lesson today.*

That is the way we see it.

Day 26: Do You Show Up to Love or to be Liked?

"Now these three remain: faith, hope and love. But the greatest of these is love." 1 Corinthians 13:13

At the end of this life, it is not the words we speak or the accomplishments we have achieved that matter but how devoutly we lived. If we show up to be liked, acknowledged or recognized we dilute our ability to remember we are complete in God, lacking nothing.

If we show up to love and serve we ignite our remembrance of our unique value and soul's purpose on earth. Fill up with God in order to give God to those around you.

Don't show up to be liked, show up to love. The difference between the two ignites inner conflict or confidence and the choice is yours.

Dear God,

My desire to be liked by other people is fueled by my own insecurities. Resurrect my one source of constant confidence: my knowing that you will never leave me or forsake me, that if you are for me, nothing can be against me. It is your favor that I want to seek over the favor of the world.

Pearl of Hope:

A desire to be right, liked or understood wreaks havoc in relationships. Embrace different perspectives without judgment. Build bridges of connection with love and confidence.

That is the way we see it.

Day 27: Your Attitude is Your Closest Friend or Worst Enemy

"Be joyful always, pray continually, give thanks in all circumstances; for this is God's will for you in Christ Jesus." 1 Thessalonians 5:16-18

Stress or peace is a direct result of your choice of attitude. Your attitude is either your best friend or your worst enemy AND the choice is yours...Choose wisely, your life experience depends on it.

Know that whenever you are hungry, angry, lonely (feeling under appreciated, unseen, dis-connected), tired or sick your attitude will be more vulnerable to negativity.

Nothing thrives in a state of war. Accept yourself right where you are at and choose love, grace, kindness and faith in the midst of it all.

Take care of your bodily needs, honor the BRAC (basic rest activity cycle of the brain). Your brain is ON 90 min and rests 20...weave breaks and self care into your day and you increase the odds that you will show up with a positive attitude towards life.

Remember you are not a victim to a bad attitude unless you choose to be. Take back your ability to show up in life with a positive out-look, your life experienced unfolds from this choice.

Dear God,

I pray for the grace today to be able to maintain a spirit of joy, a prayerful state of mind and a grateful response to every situation that unfolds before me.

Pearl of Hope:

Are you having a pity party, depressed or discouraged?

Try this:

Go out and find some place you can dream and connect with almighty God. Take a break from the routine that seems to be holding you back. Find a place that inspires you, where you can meditate on His word and allow your faith to elevate to the next level. You can do hard things.

That is the way we see it.

Day 28: Do You Lie for Greatness?

Knowing that I come from a long line of fly-fisher people, I wanted to impress my family members. I went fly fishing alone and I caught one very small rainbow trout. As I walked home, I pondered the situation and by the time I opened my mouth it had grown to 20 lbs. When questioned, I backed up my lie for greatness each time.

Have you ever lied for greatness? I woke up thinking how many times I have done this in my life: Lied for Greatness.

As human beings, we lie or distort the truth because we are afraid: afraid of failure or success, that we don't measure up, that we are not enough just as we are, fear of what others will think or say if we speak the truth, fear of not getting what we feel we need in order to completely love and accept ourselves and/or feel accomplished and successful or simply afraid that we won't get our desired outcome.

Have you ever made a statement that you know is false yet you find the words tumbling out of your mouth before you can stop them?
This is a perfect example of what happens when the drug of approval overtakes your moral compass in life.

When your desire to be seen, acknowledged, recognized and approved of exceeds your inner knowing that you are enough just as you are, that God delights in your uniqueness, you become vulnerable to this stress producing energy leak.

Keep watch on this one, it's a creepy little reptile that slithers its way into your choice of verbiage.

Basically it dilutes your character, authenticity and integrity leaving you back peddling as you attempt to regain your ground.

As I was doing an examination of consciousness over my time life concerning this topic a particular scene popped up:

Ruthless honesty will set you free, first and foremost with yourself then within relationships (personal and professional).

Speak the truth in love. This gives you opportunity to honor & ground your value & worth: *I am willing to love and accept myself no matter what surrounds me in life.*

How would your choice of words shift if you knew that you were enough just as you are?

Dear God,

I am beautifully and wonderfully created in your image, lacking nothing; More of you today and less of me. Grant me the courage to speak the truth in love even in the face of possible rejection.

Pearl of Hope:

6 Qualities Help Us in Our Thought Life:

1. *Tell the truth.*
2. *Give reverence to what is worthy.*
3. *Do what is right.*
4. *Practice moderation.*
5. *Promote peacefulness.*
6. *Leave a legacy of integrity.*

That is the way we see it.

Day 29: Ground Your Identity in God

When the soldiers came to collect Jesus for the crucifixion, he knew why they had come yet did not shrink back from his identity (John 18:4-7):

"Jesus, knowing all that was going to happen to him, went out and asked them, "Who is it you want?"
"Jesus of Nazareth," they replied.
"I am he," Jesus said

Anxiety begins to dilute our sense of identity when we consciously consent to fear, doubt and worry. When we shrink back from who we are for the sake of avoiding negative reactions, we lose focus on our purpose and mission in life.

Dear God,

Thank you for filling me with the grace to stand firm in the person you have called me to be in this world. When asked by others who I am and what I believe, I rejoice that I have the ability to speak with the same confidence that Jesus had in the face of adverse reactions.

Help me to declare who you have created me to be with confidence in every situation that unfolds before me this week... I am who I am.

Pearl of Hope:

Remember to make efforts to love in the midst of storms.

That is the way we see it

Day 30: The Savior Complex

"In his heart a man plans his course, but the Lord determines his steps." Proverbs 16:9

As I stood by the bedside holding the hand of a dear friend of mine this past weekend, who is about to transition into the heavenly realms, I encountered the reality of this statement: Grace is Uploaded NOW, not in the past or the future.

I went to spend time with the MC's (Missionaries of Charity, Mother Teresa's nuns) on Friday night to gain some insight and perspective as I continually find myself at the bedside of close friends who are leaving this earth because of the same disease I conquered.

Sister Rosily worked with Mother Teresa in Calcutta India and helped many people transition from this life into the hands of God. She said: "So you do not grow weary remember that these people belong to God so carry them to God, with your words remind them that Jesus loves them and walks with them in the valley. You are not here to save people from their circumstances, you are here to love them through it all and guide them always to God."

Dear God, grant me the grace and wisdom to remember my purpose on earth. Give me the strength to lean into the prayer of serenity as I accept the things I cannot change and move with courage to change the things I can along with the wisdom to know the difference. More of You God; less of me.

Pearl of Hope:

We all need healthy boundaries. Explore taking full responsibility to implement healthy behaviors, including positive thinking. Unhealthy behavior patterns, such as the inability to implement healthy boundaries, may have emerged from past pain, abuse or trauma. Boundary conflicts perhaps initiated out of negative experiences, however, they are our responsibility. God has woven within us the ability to set healthy boundaries. Many times we allow our limit to be crossed because of the fear of rejection, the disease to please or the drug of approval.

Seek out connections that nurture safe, grace filled and truthful relationships. Start with the face you see in the mirror. As you stay the course with better choices and supportive people, you will naturally build a sense of self-restraint that can truly become a part of your character for life.

That is the way we see it

Day 31: Animal Planet Moments

"Praise be to the God and Father of our Lord Jesus Christ, the Father of compassion and the God of all comfort, who comforts us in a our troubles, so that we can comfort those in any trouble with the comfort we ourselves have received from God." 2 Corinthians 1:3-4

Chances are, if you are still wearing your *earth suit* you have encountered an overtly unhappy human being. Perhaps the display of unhappiness comes in their intonation, body language and/or choice of words.

Understand that when people find themselves in an Animal Planet moment, kicking and screaming their way through the day, it is simply because they forget they are loved, safe and connected to their creator.

Exercise your soul in the way of love this week. The next time you find yourself in the space of an overtly cranky person, deliberately choose to increase your expressions of kindness and love.

This is a wonderfully powerful practice. I have seen first hand how my choice for love & kindness resurrects love & kindness in the person to which it is directed. Love evokes more love; kindness evokes more kindness.

Step into the emotional state of behavior you desire to experience from people you encounter this week.

Dear God,

I admit I have played the roll of the lioness attacking the zebra in my path. I have also experienced the attack of the lions in life. Help me to remember that love wins out in the end. As quickly as possible, move me back into the healing space of love and kindness. My greatest place of inner peace lies in my choice to step out of judgment, defensive behavior and ugly talk. I am always safe and connected in you, lacking nothing.

Pearl of Hope:

Resist the urge to give more authority to other people's opinions and behavior than to God for your sense of safety and connection in this world.

That is the way we see it.

About the Authors

Lauren E Miller is a world-renowned stress relief expert, award winning international bestselling author/speaker and founder of Stress Solutions University.com receiving national recognition in Redbook, Ladies Home Journal, Family Circle, Success, CNBC, MSNBC, Lifetime and Discovery along with the International Journal of Healing and Care.

With 18 years of intensive extended education in the areas of anxiety relief and stress reduction as well as youth and adult ministries, Lauren equips men and women worldwide with the skill-sets to step into personal excellence and inner peace. Lauren is a certified Master Business Coach and Master NLP Practitioner and holds her Advanced Training Certificate in EFT, energy psychology modalities that lead to profound inner transformation.

She holds a 2nd degree black belt from the World Tae Kwon Do Federation. She has conquered two top life stressors at the same time: advanced cancer and divorce. Her 4th Best Selling Book: 5 Minutes to Stress Relief, Career Press/New Page Books, is published in 8 countries. Lauren is a featured content writer for HR.com and has produced 9 CD/DVD products that address specific life stressors/anxieties and how to release them with ease including LEVITY: a light/sound therapy product that increases endorphins/serotonin 25%, boosting mood and memory naturally.

Lauren is a part of the Avanoo.com team as a content development featured author. For more details please

visit Lauren's website: **www.LaurenEMiller.com**

Explore Lauren's 30-Day Three-Minute Daily Excellence & Wellness Programs: Stress; Relationships; Cancer Conquerors Mindset; Stress Solutions for the Soul =>

StressSolutionsUniversity.com => Making Life Style Stress Solutions Easy & Sustainable for You

Go To: **StressSolutionsUniversity.com**
Lighten Up => Let Go & Live

StressSolutionsMadeEasy.com => Levity Light/Sound Product: Boost Serotonin/Endorphins Naturally 25%

Edie Hand is a businesswoman, international speaker and author, media personality, filmmaker, and Mom. She has authored and been a part of authoring over twenty-five books.

Photo by Josh Fogel
www.joshfogel.com

Edie is the founder of the "Women of True Grit" franchise that encourages women to share their stories of how they navigated through hard things to find beautiful situations. Edie has partnered with NBC/WAFF 48 Gray Television of Huntsville, ABC 33/40 Sinclair television of Birmingham, Alabama and Alabama Public Television to bring heartfelt and educational stories to help women and students not feel alone as they face the seasons of life. Stay tuned for "Women of True Grit Pearls of Hope" programming on Tuscaloosa's Town Square Media's Christian and country radio stations. Available now through Edie Hand Foundation and Alabama Sports Foundation of Montgomery is the "Grit:101 For Teens" program. Additionally, there are programs for college students and community leaders.

She was the CEO of a full-service ad company, Hand 'N Hand Advertising, in Birmingham and

Daphne, Alabama for over thirty years. In recent years she partnered with her Hollywood actor/businessman son, Linc Hand, to form Hand N Hand Entertainment to continue her writing for film, television, radio, and podcasts. Edie also founded the Edie Hand Foundation over fifteen years ago in memory of her three, young Blackburn brothers to help pay life forward with acts of kindness to others with broken hearts. Edie is a four-time Cancer survivor and understands living with chronic illness, but always finds the grit to keep moving onward and upward. She learned how to turn hard things into beautiful situations.

She also comes from a wonderful family heritage of songwriting, acting, and music from the Hood-Hacker-Presley Family. Her legendary cousin was Elvis Presley and she learned firsthand about paying life forward through charities in one's community. Edie Hand (formerly Edith Blackburn Hand) is an alumnus of the University of North Alabama. She and her friend George Lindsey founded scholarships for students pursuing a career in theater or communications. Edie lives near Birmingham, Alabama but her heart is in Hollywood, California with her only son actor, Linc Hand, and his singer/songwriter wife Victoria Renee Hand.

To learn more about Edie, her books, the charities she supports, and her speaking topics or arranging a speaking engagment or a GRIT:101 Teen Team visit, or a corporate/college leadership workshop visit her websites:

www.EdieHand.com
www.WomenofTrueGrit.org
www.EdieHandFoundation.org
Grit.ihupapp.org

A Special Thank You to:
Mark Dubis, CEO of The Dubis Group for helping to bring Pearls of Hope with Stress Solutions for the Soul to life.
www.dubisgroup.com

Edie Hand's
WomenofTrueGrit.org

Program for teens. Visit
EdieHandFoundation.org
Partnered with
ASF Foundation
Alabama state games
Sharing life skills for teens and
college students
Laura Burt Creel
https://www.asffoundation.org/

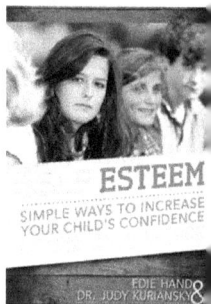

Self Esteem
Edie Hand &
Dr. Judy Kuriansky

Grit: 101

These are the strings that form our unique pearls of life.

White
Purity of Faith
and Second Chances

Red
Passion
Show respect for others

Pink
Happiness

Green
Finances/freedom to find peace

Silver
Wisdom

Blue
Courage/Allowing to trust

Black
A Path through Grief

Gold
Self-Esteem/Endurance

Purple
Leadership/Creativity to
find better choices

Teal
Total Wellness for
mind and body

Learning to listen to others voices can help you make
better choices for tomorrows to come.

WomenofTrueGrit.org

EdieHand.com

Pearls on. Swords Up.

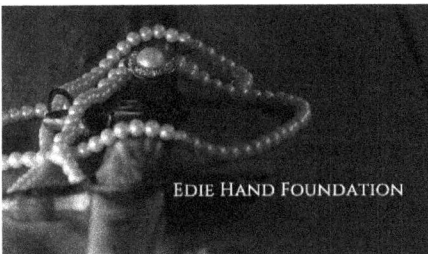

EDIE HAND FOUNDATION

www.ingramcontent.com/pod-product-compliance
Lightning Source LLC
Chambersburg PA
CBHW061156040426
42445CB00013B/1698